Iran

Afghanistan

Pakistan

ALI'S STORY...

A **real-life** account of his journey from Afghanistan

Created by
Salvador Maldonado
and Andy Glynne

First published in 2014 by Wayland

Text and Illustrations © Mosaic Films 2014

Wayland, 338 Euston Road, London NW1 3BH

Wayland Australia, Level 17/207, Kent Street, Sydney, NSW 2000

Mosaic Films, Shacklewell Lane, London E8 2EZ

Created by Andy Glynne & Salvador Maldonado
Artwork by Tom Clohosy Cole
Additional artwork by Laura Bird

Editor: Debbie Foy
Designer: Sophie Wilkins

Dewey ref: 362.7'7914'092-dc23

ISBN 978 0 7502 7887 4
eBook ISBN 978 0 7502 9337 2
Lib eBook ISBN 978 0 7502 7892 8

Printed in China

10 9 8 7 6 5 4 3 2 1

Wayland is a division of Hachette Children's Books,
an Hachette UK company.

www.hachette.co.uk

ALI'S STORY...

My name is Ali.

This is the story of my journey
from Afghanistan.

WAYLAND
www.waylandbooks.co.uk

My family and I lived in Afghanistan.
There were mountains there and lots of dust.
Most people weren't rich and they
didn't have houses. Instead
they lived in tents.

There was always so much fighting going on,
but the war started to get worse.

There were lots of helicopters in
the sky and tanks started to
bomb our town and cities.

Sometimes I
would look out
of the window and
see the fighting going on.

It made me very scared,
but also really sad.

The war got so
bad that my grandma
decided that we should all
pack our bags and go
to a safer place
in Europe.

When we got to the airport, the officials let my grandma in, then me, but they turned my mum and dad away!

They said that my parents did not have passports and so they had to go back home.

My grandma and I got on the plane.
We thought my mum and
dad were on another
plane following
behind us.

My grandma and I were
safe in this strange new country but
we didn't know what had happened to

Sometimes I dreamt that it was my mum who picked me up from school, and walked me home.

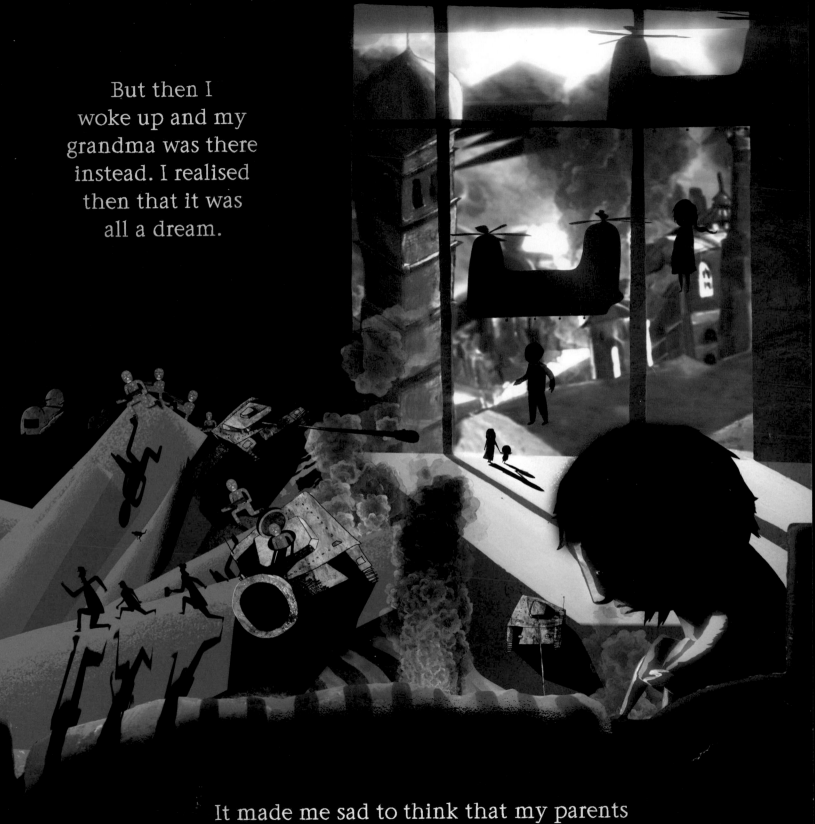

But then I woke up and my grandma was there instead. I realised then that it was all a dream.

It made me sad to think that my parents were back in Afghanistan among all the war and the fighting.

I dreamt about them all the time
and I cried every night. It was like the
bones in my body were broken.

Sometimes
I felt angry, but
most of the time
I felt really sad.

Sometimes I got
embarrassed
when I didn't
know the word
for something.

At the beginning
I sat in the corner of the
playground watching
all the other
kids play.

Sometimes people would
ask me to play with them,
and soon I had a group of friends
that I played football
with at school.

I really love drawing and everyone
was amazed by my pictures.

Every day I would draw a
special picture to show
people at school.

Sometimes it would be a picture
of my whole family, or just my
mum and dad, me, or a superhero
(because I really like superheroes)!

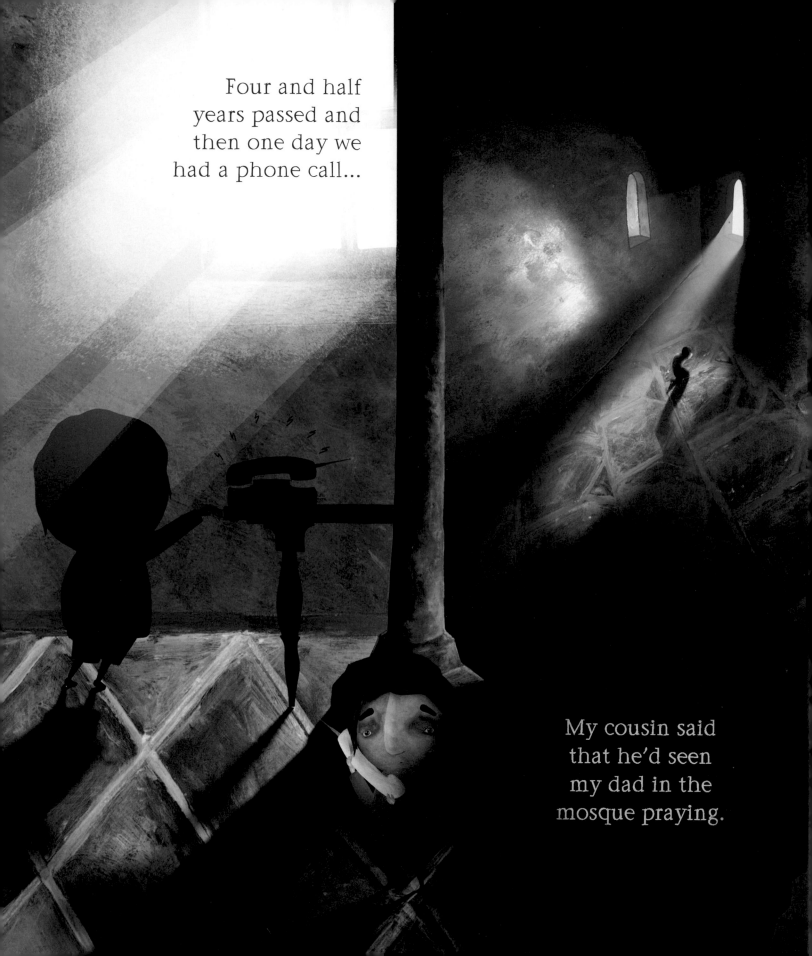

Four and half
years passed and
then one day we
had a phone call...

My cousin said
that he'd seen
my dad in the
mosque praying.

Then, he handed the phone to my mum and dad and I talked to them for the first time in years.

It made me feel so happy.

My biggest wish is that my mum and dad would come to this country.

It feels like it's going to happen
sometime soon, but I get upset
when I think about them and
wish they could come
right now.

I can't wait for that day.

The complete **SEEKING REFUGE** series.

Real-life testimonies of young refugees fleeing their homelands.

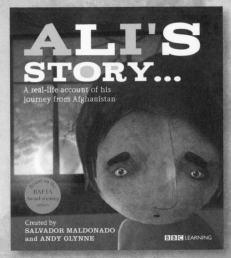

9780750278874
eBk ISBN 978 0 7502 9337 2

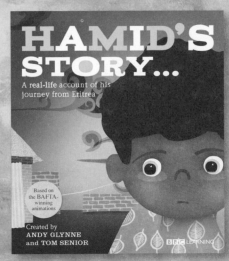

9780750278904
eBk ISBN 978 0 7502 9348 8

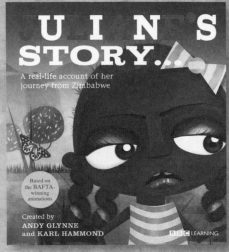

9780750278898
eBk ISBN 978 0 7502 9347 1

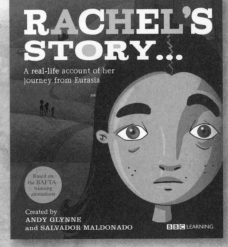

9780750278881
eBk ISBN 978 0 7502 9374 7

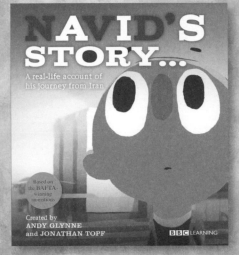

9780750278911
eBk ISBN 978 0 7502 9373 0

Available only from WAYLAND

WAYLAND
www.waylandbooks.co.uk